SWU-600-003

HORSEMEN IN
THE 16TH &17TH C.

✶

BY JACOB DE GHEYN II
& A. DE BRUYN

Series curated by
Luca Stefano Cristini

SOLDIERSHOP PUBLISHING

AUTHOR

Jacob de Gheyn II (1565 - 1629). Dutch renommated artist and engraver was born in Antwerp and died in The Hague (NL). He was a pupil of Hendrick Goltzius in Haarlem. He is one of the circle of engravers of the Mannerist school like Matham, Saenredam and Goltzius. De Gheyn made also interesting prints on military items. His series of military exercises, subjets of our book is widely known.

Abraham de Bruyn (c.1539, Antwerp - 1587, Cologne) Flemish engraver. He established himself at Cologne about the year 1577. He is ranked among the Little Masters, on account of his plates being usually very small. He engraved in the manner of Wierix, and worked entirely with the graver, in a neat and formal style, but his drawing is far from correct. It is believed that he worked also as a goldsmith.

PUBLISHING'S NOTE

NOTE ABOUT BOOK PRINTING BEFORE 1925

LICENSES COMMONS

ACKNOWLEDGEMENTS

A Special Thanks to Rijkmuseum and other institutions for their kindly permission or policy to use some images of his archives, collections or books used in our book.

Title: **HORSEMEN IN 16TH & 17TH C. - by Jacob de Gheyn II** & A. De Bruyn
Series edit & curated by Luca S. Cristini. First edition by Soldiershop. February 2017
Cover & Art Design: Luca S. Cristini. Plates re-colorations by Anna Cristini.
ISBN code: 978-88-93271554
Published by Soldiershop publishing, via Padre Davide, 7 - 24050 Zanica (BG) ITALY. www.soldiershop.com

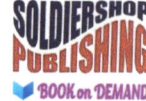

HORSEMEN IN
16TH & 17TH C.

BY JACOB DE GHEYN II
& ABRAHAM DE BRUYN

DIVERSARVM
GENTIVM ARMATVRA
EQVESTRIS.

Vbi fere Europæ Asiæ atq̃
Africæ equitandi ratio
propria expressa
est.

1575

Abrahamo Bruynus Excude.

HISTORICAL ILLUSTRATIONS OF EUROPEAN KNIGHTS AT HORSE

The celebrated Dutch artist Jacob de Gheyn (1565-1625), famous author of 1608 masterpiece, named: *Maniement d'armes, d'arquebuses, mousquet et piques* in French language, and *Exercice of armes* in England. Already published by Soldiershop in the first volume of this series.

He is also the creator of a fine series of 22 numbered prints titled: *"De ruiterschool"* (the equestrian school") composed by a frontispiece, 20 prints in which one or a few different types (most armor) of riders are shown, and a print of a cavalry skirmish.

The second part of our book presents the artwork of Abraham De Bruyn (1539-1587), a famous Flemish Engraver. He is ranked among the Little Masters on account of his plates being usually very small.

The De Bruyn series is based on several European knights and horsemen in the 16th century.

Above and beyond its intrinsic historic interest, the volume presents a meticulously accurate portrait of uniforms and weapons of the era of Netherlands and Europe, in addition to the aesthetic appeal of the remarkable engravings of this great artist!

◄ *Frontispiece of "Diversarum gentium armatura equestris", Keulen, 1577 by A.De Bruyn*

CONTENTS

JACOB DE GHEYN II AND THE DUTCH MILITARY ART IN 17th CENTURY

De Gheyn was born in Antwerp in 1565 and received his first training directly from his father, Jacob de Gheyn I, a glass painter, engraver, and draftsman. In 1585, he moved to Haarlem, where he studied under Hendrik Goltzius for the next five years, and of which become the most important pupil. He is one of the great artist of the circle of engravers of the Mannerist school like Matham, Saenredam and Goltzius.

In this years he absorbed Goltzius's sinuous linear technique, which appeared in de Gheyn's early engravings. Mannerism is the style between the late renaissance and early baroque. Typical is a certain exaggerated tortion of the figures, often with thick fingers and cheeks, and small mouth with filled lips. The scene is mostly placed in an imaginary searched landscape with a prominent tree with twisted branches under a tormented sky. This is the cultivation of the art feeling of late 16th century.

After Harlem, Jacob moved again, to Leiden, in the middle of the 1590s. His work attracted the attention of wealthy sponsors, and his first commission was for an engraving of the Siege of Geertruidenberg from Maurice of Nassau, Prince of Orange.

This event from March 27 to June 24, 1593, had been more of a demonstration of power by Prince Maurits, than an actual war, and had even attracted tourists. As a publicity stunt, the siege and its subsequent engraving were successful in propagating an image of Prince Maurits as an able general.

Around 1600, de Gheyn abandoned engraving, and focused on painting and etching. Moving to The Hague in 1605, he was employed often by Dutch royalty, designing a garden in the Buitenhof for Prince Maurice of Orange which featured the two first grottoes in the Netherlands. After Prince Maurice's death in 1625, de Gheyn worked for his brother, Prince Frederick Henry. De Gheyn painted some of the earliest female nudes, vanitas, and floral still lifes in Dutch art.

He is credited with creating over 1,500 drawings, including landscapes and natural history illustrations. While in Amsterdam, in the years 1607/1608, he made 117 designs for engraved illustrations in a military training manual to aid the Dutch fight for independence from Spain. This military manual is: *The Exercise of Armes* presented in this book.

De Gheyn married Eva Stalpaert van der Wiele of Mechelen in 1595. His son, Jacob de Gheyn III, was born in 1596, and grew to become an engraver in his own right, as well as the subject of a portrait by Rembrandt. De Gheyn died in The Hague in 1629.

DE RUITERSCHOOL (THE EQUESTRIAN SCHOOL)

Our collection of renaissance knights realized by Jacob de Gheyn is composed by a formidable series of masterpieces.

The first plate is the frontispiece with a Latin text in a cartouche. Left next to a figure in armor (a rider, according to the reins which he holds in his hand), right next to a soldier without armor; under the text a skull. This first print is part of a series of 22 numbered prints: a frontispiece, 20 prints in which one or a few different types (most armor) of riders are shown, and a print of a cavalry skirmish. Finally in the last plate there is a cavalry skirmish near a fortress. In the foreground left there are two trumpeters, two right spear horsemen. The center plans a number of horsemen (leaders of the cavalry).

The second part of this book is based on 77 plates of world's knights realized in the late XVI century by the Flemish artist Abraham de Bruyn. These great plates are Presented for the first time, in full colour.

▲ *Allegorical artwork on the hard soldier's life by J.De Gheyn - Rijksmuseum, Amsterdam*

DIVERSARUM GENTIUM ARMATURA EQUESTRIS 1577

Abraham de Bruyn Engraver and publisher. Born in Antwerp, where active from 1565, but often moved. c.1576-8 and again after 1585 in Cologne where he died. Father of Nicolaes de Bruyn.

Much work for Plantin Published several books: *"Imperii ac Sacerdotii Ornatus, Diversarum item gentium vestitus"* (Cologne, 1578); the our *"Diversarum gentium armatura equestris"* (Cologne, 1577) and *"Omnium paene gentium imagines"* (Antwerp, 1581).

Equitum descripcio, quomodo equestres copie, nostra hac aetate, in sua armatura, per cunttas, videlicet Europae, Asiae et Affrice, nationes in re militare sese habent nunc primum, & hactenus nusqz, impressioni tradita : nonnullis tamen interpositis autea [sic] impressis,

Note to the plates

1- Horse and rider to the right. The horse is galloping while the rider, in typical German dressed, blowing his horn or trumpet.

2- Horse and rider to the right. The horse is in step. The German clad horseman carrying a lance. About all the prints has a German team and a Latin inscription.

3- Horse and rider left. The horse is galloping. The soldier is wearing German clothes style.

4- Horse and rider left. The horse is galloping. The German rider dressed wearing a gun in his hand. The print has a German team and a Latin inscription.

5- Horse and rider left. The horse is galloping. The rider is wearing German clothes.

6- Horse and rider left. The horse is in step. The young German rider carries a mace in his hand.

7- Horse and rider to the right. The horse rears. The German rider carries a mace in his hand and a black armor.

8- Horse and rider to the right. The horse is in step. The German rider carrying a lance in his hand and is harnessed.

9- Horse and rider left. The horse is in step. The drummer, in German dressed, beats on a drum.

10- Horse and rider to the right. The horse rears. The German rider commander carrying a baton in his hand.

11- Horse and rider left. The horse rears. The German prince wearing a small whip in his hand.

12- Horse and rider left. The horse is in step. On the horse a Dutch prince.

13- Horse and rider to the right. The horse is in step. The Dutch noblewoman riding sidesaddle and a whip in the hands.

14- Horse and rider to the right. The horse is in step. The Dutch master has a riding crop.

15- Horse and rider to the right. The horse is in step. The Dutch squire has a whip in his hand.

16- Horse and rider to the right. The horse is in step. The Dutch nobleman has a falcon on hand

17- Horse and rider to the right. Knight wearing armor and a lance in his hand.

18- Horse and rider left. The horse rears. The Dutch commander has a baton in his hand.

19- Horse and rider left. The horse is in step. The Dutch rider dressed with a gun in hand.

20- Horse and rider to the right. The horse is galloping. The Dutch rider has a carbine in hand.

21- Horse and rider left. The horse in gallop. The Dutch Lancer has a lance in the hand and is harnessed.

22- Horse and rider to the right. The horse rears. On the horse the Duke of Anjou. In his hand he holds a baton.

23- Horse and rider left. The horse is in step. On the horse a French nobleman with a riding crop in hand.

24- Horse and rider to the right. The horse is galloping. The French rider has a gun in his hands.

25- Horse and rider to the right. The horse rears. The French rider has a spear in his hands and is fully harnessed.

26- Horse and rider left. The horse is in step and adds two French noblemen on his back. The front squire has a riding crop.

27- Horse and rider to the right. The horse is in step. The rider is identified by his clothes as French councilor. According to the accompanying text, he is heading to the Paris parliament.

28- Horse and rider left. The horse rears. The Italian dressed squire has a whip in his hands.

29- Horse and rider to the right. The horse is in step. The rider is fully harnessed and secured a lance. He is dressed in Italian style.

30- Horse and rider left. The horse is in step. The rider wears a long robe and matching clothes.

31- Horse and rider to the right. The horse is galloping. The rider has the uniform of the British Yeomen of the Guard, the guards of the Queen of England. In his hand a gun.

32- Horse and rider left. The horse is galloping. The rider is Irish and riding the horse without a saddle or bridle. He is holding a bow.

33- Horse and rider left. The horse is in step. The rider is noble dressed in Spanish style.

34- Horse and rider left. The horse is in step. The rider is dressed as a Spanish councilor and a whip in his hand.

35- Horse and rider to the right. The horse is in step. The Spanish rider wears clothes and is holding a gun.

36- Horse and rider left. The horse is in step. The Spanish rider has a long raincoat on. In his hand a gun.

37- Horse and rider to the right. The horse is galloping. The Spanish picador has a spear in his hands.

38- Horse and rider to the right. The horse rears. The Polish rider wears dress and holding a spear in his hand.

39- Horse and rider to the right. The horse is galloping. The nobleman has Hungarian clothes and a spear in his hand.

40- The cartouche containing the image of a horse and rider to the left. The horse stands still. The rider wears Hungarian clothes and has a spear in his hand. On his back he carries a shield.

41- Horse and rider to the right. The horse is in step. The Polish rider is wearing clothes and an ax in his hand.

42- Two horses and riders left. The horses are in step. The riders are dressed and wearing in Polish Style. A trumpet in hand. The second rider blows his trumpet.

43- Two horses riders left. The horses are in step. The riders are dressed in Polish style. One blows on a flute, the other beats on a drum.

44- Two horses and riders left. The horses are in step. The riders are dressed in Polish style. They both carry a banner.

45- Two horses and riders left. The horses are in step. The riders are dressed in Polish style.

46- Horse and rider left. The horse is in step. The rider was dressed in royal Russian fashion.

47- Horse and rider to the right. The horse is in step. The Russian rider is dressed and wearing a morning star and a drum.

48- Horse and rider to the right. The horse is in step. The rider is a Moscovite noble and Russian dressed. He holds a lance in his hand.

▲ XVI century guards, gentleman and notable people by A.De Bruyn

49- Horse and rider to the right. The horse is galloping. The rider is Russian dressed and has an ax in his hands.

50- Horse and rider left. The horse is galloping. The rider is Russian dressed and has a spear in his hands.

51- Horse and rider to the right. The horse is galloping. The rider was Baltic dressed and has a lance in his hand.

52- Horse and rider left. The horse is galloping. The rider is a Tartar and a morning star in a hand.

53- The cartouche containing the image of a horse and rider to the right. The horse is galloping. The rider is dressed in Romanian style and has a spear and a shield in his hands.

54- Horse and rider left. The horse is in step. The rider's Sultan Murad III. He has an Ottoman robe and a scepter in his hand.

55- The cartouche containing the image of a horse and rider to the left. The horse is in step. The rider is dressed like an Ottoman court man.

56- Horse and rider left. The horse rears. Grand vizier Ibrahim Pasha Ottoman style dressed and has an ax in his hands.

57- Cartouche depicting a horse and rider to the right. The horse is in step. The rider is the leader of the Janissaries, the elite troops of the Ottoman court. He has a baton in his hand.

58- Cartouche depicting a horse and rider to the left. The horse is in step. The rider is a lieutenant of the Janissaries, the elite troops of the Ottoman court. He has an ax in his hand.

▲ *XVI century foot soldier by A.De Bruyn*

59- Cartouche depicting a horse and rider to the right. The horse is in step. The rider is a captain of the Jannissaries, the elite troops of the Ottoman court. He has a spear in his hand.

60- Horse and rider to the right. The horse is in step. The rider is dressed in Ottoman style. He has a shield in his hand.

61- Horse and rider left. The horse is in step. The rider is an adventurer who is part of the Ottoman army. He has a shield and a spear in his hand.

62- Cartouche depicting a horse and rider to the right. The horse is in step. The rider is dressed like a Persian nobleman. He has a ax in his hand.

63- Cartouche with image of horse and rider to the right. The horse is galloping. The rider is dressed like a Persian soldier. He has a spear in his hand.

64- Cartouche depicting a horse and rider to the left. The horse is galloping. The rider is a Mamluk soldier. He has a spear in his hand.

65- Cartouche depicting a horse and rider to the left. The horse is in step. The rider is a Mamluk soldier. He has a shield and a spear in his hands.

66- Cartouche depicting a horse and rider to the right. The horse is galloping. The rider is an Arab officer. He has a spear in his hand.

67- Cartouche depicting a horse and rider to the right. The horse is galloping. The rider is an Arab. He rides bareback and a spear in his hand.

68- Cartouche depicting a horse and rider to the right. The horse is in step. The rider is of Moorish origin. He has a spear in his hand and riding a horse bareback.

69- Cartouche depicting a horse and rider to the right. The horse is in step. The rider is dressed as an Arab gentleman. He has a staff in his hand.

70- Cartouche depicting riders to right. Their horses are in step. The riders are recognizable by their dress as an Arab nobleman and his wife. He has a spear in his hand.

71- Cartouche depicting a horse and rider to the right. The horse stands still. The rider of Scythian origin. He has a bow in his right hand. In his left hand he holds an ax up with them impaled the head of an opponent. On his saddle even more heads hang.

72- Cartouche depicting a horse and rider to the right. The horse is galloping. The rider is Parth. He has a bow in the hands and shoot at a target behind him.

73- Cartouche depicting dromedary and two riders to the right. The dromedary in step. Two riders are of Moorish origin. One has a bow in his hands and shoot an arrow.

74- Cartouche depicting a camel and rider left. The animal is in step. Its rider was an Arab man.

75- Cartouche depicting a horse and rider to the left. The horse stands still. The rider is of Indian origin. He has a spear in his hands and carrying a large shield on the back.

76- Horse and rider left. The horse is in step. The rider was an Indian prince.

77- Elephant get right. The beast is in step. Seven Indians sitting on the elephant. Most have fixed spears or bows.

Comipedem ut brevibus deceat compescere habenis,
  Frænáq̃ tardanti liberiora dare :
Et modò per campum curvo contendere gyro,
  Et modò directis leniter ire vys:
Vt ve ensem femori, lateri ve educere selopum
  Debeat, aut hastæ tendere acumen eques.
Geÿnius hęc pariter quam vel Mars ferreus ipse
  Dicet in ære tibi tutius, et melius.

                                    HErrotzius

HGthein in, et ex,

THE
COLOUR
PLATES

1

DE GHEYN

DE RUITERSCHOOL
(THE EQUESTRIAN SCHOOL)

22

23

31

35

36

37

2

ABRAHAM DE BRUYN

"DIVERSARUM GENTIUM ARMATURA EQUESTRIS"

1577

39

Tubicen Germanus.

Ein Trometer Nach teutscher vnd dem
Brunswicher gebrauch bey dem fursten
Abraham d bruyn fecit 1575 I

Calator et honorarius puer Nobilis Germani.

Derr Adel Junger Wie fur denn grossen Hern Ryden

2.

Equestris habitus Principis Comitis, vel Baronis
Germani

Wie die Teutscher fursten Graffen und freyen Herrn rheyten.

3

Nobilis Germani habitus equestris.

Eyn Teutscher Edelman wie sie inn felt rheyden.

Equestris habitus Germanorū.

Eyn Teutscher Reyter In yhrer Kleydung ~

5

44

Equitis Gemani cacula.

Eijn Teutscher Reijter Iung ..

Eques nigrantis   armaturæ Germanorum.

Die Teutscher reüter inn schwartzer rusting.

7

Signifer equitum Germanorum.

Die reÿter fhann beÿ denn Teutschen reuteren. 8

Æneator

Die keſſel drummelſchlager.

9.

Ein oberste ober die teutsche. Præfectus Equitum Germanorum
reuter.

IO.

Princeps siue Comes Germanus.

Ein Edler Furst inn Teutflant

II

Ein Edler Fürst im Niderlant.   Princeps siue Dominus Belga.

IZ.

Nobilis apud Belgas feminæ habitus eqnestris.

Wie die Niderlansche Edelfrawen rheyten

13.

Magnatum Belgicorum vrba na atque aulica equitatio.

Wie die großen Hern in Niderlandt bey Haoff rheyden.

14

Ein Niderlanſche Iuncker.   Adoleſcens Princeps ſiue
Dominus Belga.

15.

Nobilis Belgæ aucupa-   torius habitus-

Eyn Niderlanſche edelman wie ſie mit denn walcken auſz heyten.

16.

Cataphractus eques ad decursionem comparatus.

Die thurnier Ruftung zum Ritlichen thurnier spill.

17

Militum tribuuis Belga

Eyn Niderlansche Koronell oder vbriste vber das fusuolck

18.

Ein Niderlansche reuter schutz.
Ferentarius Belga.

19 · H

Eques Belga ferentarius.

Eyn Welsche oder Niderlansche reyter genant karabin.

20.

Niderlansche lancier.   Lanceatus miles Belga.   D. 21.

Franciscus Valesius D. G. Dux Alanson⁵ Fr. Regis Franc. ZZ.

Ein Francoscher Edelmann.   Nobilis Gallus   Z3.

Eques Francus.

Eyn Franceusche reuter mitten langen rhor

z4.

Ein Francofcher Lancier. Lanceatus eques Gallus. 25.

Nobiles vel Franci vel Belga in opidis obeguitautes.

Wie die franceusche Iuncker bey haaff reyten zwey auff einem pherd.

Z 6.

Consiliarius in   Parlamento Parisiensi .

Ein Rhatsherr zu Paris im Parlement .   27.

Ein Hofiuncker inn Italia.   Nobilis Italus.   38 . .

Eques Italus.

Eyn Italianische reyter mitter lancen.

Z 9.

Ein Hofiuncker in Engelandt.   Nobilis Anglus. 30.

Reginæ Angliæ   sattelles ferentarius.

Eÿn Engelsche reÿter die auf der Kunigin von Engeland wartten.

31

Hibernus vel Irlandus eques.

Eÿn wilde Ihrlansche rheÿter.

32.

71

Ein Hiſpaniſcher hofiuncker. Aulicus nobilis Hiſpanus. 33.

Ein Hispanischer Rhatsherr. Senator Hispanus. 34.

Ein Hiſpanier ſchutz.   Ferentarius Hiſpanus.   18. M

Eques Hispanus.

Eyn Hispanische reuter mittenn langen rhor

36

Sic Hispani tauros infectantur.

Wie sie die spanier rusten die stier zu iagen. 37

Eques   Polon us.

Derr Poolsche reyter.   38.

Nobilis Hungarus.

Ein Edelman zu roß in Ungerland.

39.

Vulgaris Hungarus.

Die gemeine Vngerſche reuter ruſtung. 40.

Ein Polonischer Hofiunaker. Nobilis Polonus. 41.

Polonischer trommetter.　　Tubicen Polonus.

4 z. ▼ ▼

Typanistæ Polonorum

Equitum.

Die trummelſhlager beÿ die Polſche Reuter.

43.

Polonorum Equitum Signifere.

Die Polonischer Reuter fhann. 44

83

Polonifcher Reuter.   Equites Poloni.   48.

Groß Furst in der Moscouw .   Princeps Moscouitarum . 46.

R

Præfectus militiæ in Moscovia.

Ein Felluberste uberster beÿ die Moscouiter reuter. 47.

Nobilis Moscouita   habitu atque armis equestribus.

Eyn Edler Moscouiter in seyner rustung.   48

Moscouita cum armis equestribus.

Derr Moscouiten reÿter mit seyn kriechs waffen.

49.

Eques Ruthenus.

Derr Ruſſen reẙter.

50.

Eques ex Lithuania.

Ein Litauwer reüter.

51.

Eques Tartarus.

Eyn Tartarisch reyter.

52

Eques Walachus.

Ein Reuter auß der Walachi

Soltanus Murathes   Turc. Imp.

Sultan Murat Derr ijetziger Turckischer Keyser   54.

Summmus et religionis et legum Iudex in Turia

Cadilesquer seijnt Oberste Richter Beij den Turcken 55

Der uberste Vifir Baſſa.   56:
Præfectus militiæ, ſiue Baſcha, in Turcia. ⬛⬛.z.

Alga Iani zerorum in Turcia Tribunus.

Alga Ist ein Oberste vber die Janitzer 57

Mille Ianizerorum.   Tribuni legatus.

Chechaia protogero Oder leutenant Vber. 1000.
Janitzer   158

Ianizerorum Centurio.

59.

Boluck baſsi ſint haupleut vber 100 Janitzer.

Ein Turckscher reuter.   Eques Turcus.   6 ð.

Emiſſarius.

Der waech hals. Oder abenturer Delli genant

61

Perſa nobilis.

Ein Edler Perſianer   GZ.

Ein Perſianer reuter
Eques Perſa.

65

Marmalucus seu apostata.

Der Mammeluck sint verleungde khristen
64

Mammalucus ex Aegypto.

Ein Mammeluck in Egiptia   G 5.

Magister equitum in Arabia.

Ein Uberste der reuter in Arabia

6.6

Eques siluestris Arabiæ.

Ein reuter in dem Wilden Arabia

67.

Eques   *Maurus in Algeriano regno.*

Ein Morrhen reuter zu Algier. 68.

Arabs præcipuæ dignitatis.

Ein großen arabischer Herr auß Egipten

69

Cayro nobilis vna cum sua vxore.

Ein Edler zu alkeÿr mit seiner frauw. 70.

Schyta.

Ein reuter auß den land Schithia
371.

Parthus,

Ein reuter auß Perthia

7 Z

Bini Mauri in camelo, quem dromada nominant, equitantes.

Zweien mhoren reuter auff denn dromedarij

73

In camelo equitans Asia ticus.

Ein asianische reuter auff denn kamelthier
74

A Narsinga eques Indens.

Ein Indianer reuter zu Narsinga   7

Ein Indianischer fürst zu Narsinga
Princeps in Narsinga.   76.

Septeni milites in elephanto Indico.

Siben mann reijten auff ein Hellffant im krieg 77.

Est, non est: turbant concordia fœdera mundi,
  Nec non, ad priscum cuncta chaos revocant.
Fronte ferunt punctum: paribus stant cominus armis
  Claudicat alteruter; nec movet usque gradum.

Assiduo servet Capitolia Terminus unus;
  Nunc geminus curram regnat in orbe deus?
Di date, vel Parcæ potius moriatur ut hocum
  Alter: sic mundo parta quies fuerit.   C.D.

SOLDIERS, WEAPONS & UNIFORMS ALREADY PUBLISHED
(TITLES ALREADY PUBLISHED)

SOLDIERS, WEAPONS & UNIFORMS OF XVI-XVII CENTURY
(TITLES ALREADY PUBLISHED)

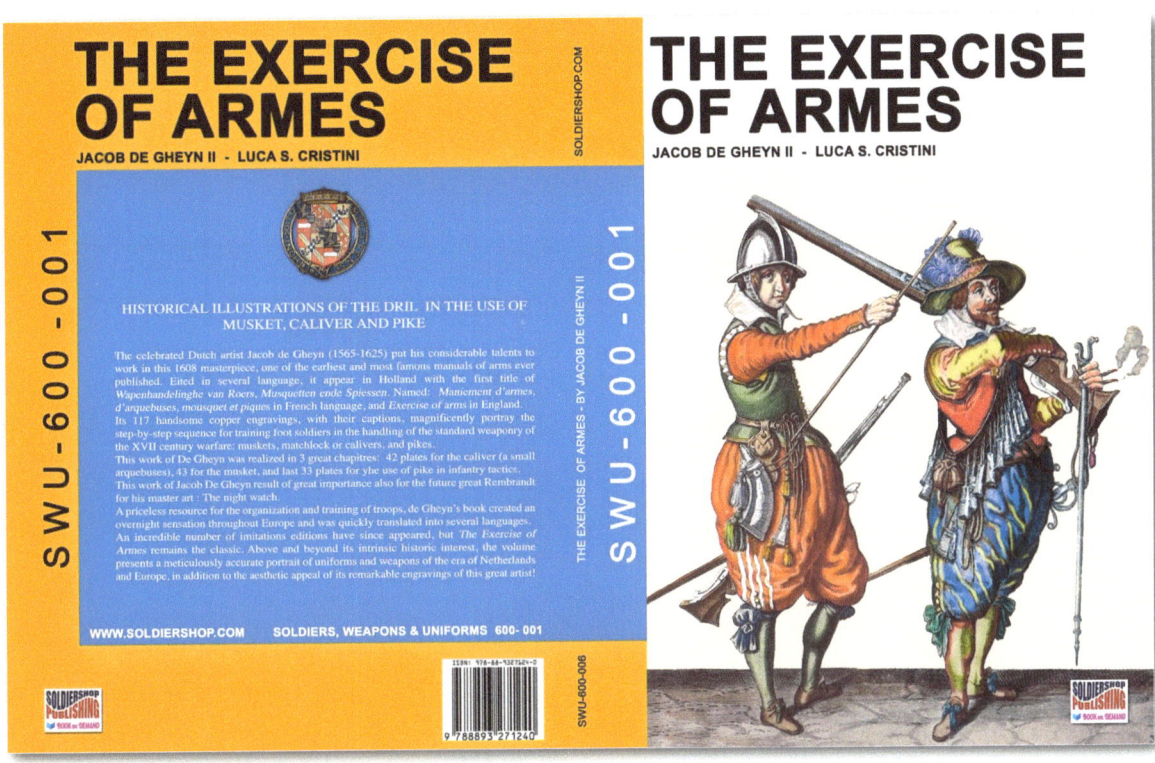

THE EXERCISE OF ARMES
JACOB DE GHEYN II - LUCA S. CRISTINI

SWU-600-001

SOLDIERSHOP.COM

THE EXERCISE OF ARMES - BY JACOB DE GHEYN II

SWU-600-001

HISTORICAL ILLUSTRATIONS OF THE DRIL IN THE USE OF MUSKET, CALIVER AND PIKE

The celebrated Dutch artist Jacob de Gheyn (1565-1625) put his considerable talents to work in this 1608 masterpiece, one of the earliest and most famous manuals of arms ever published. Eited in several language, it appear in Holland with the first title of *Wapenhandelinghe van Roers, Musquetten ende Spiessen*. Named: *Maniement d'armes, d'arquebuses, mousquet et piques* in French language, and *Exercise of arms* in England.
Its 117 handsome copper engravings, with their captions, magnificently portray the step-by-step sequence for training foot soldiers in the handling of the standard weaponry of the XVII century warfare: muskets, matchlock or calivers, and pikes.
This work of De Gheyn was realized in 3 great chapitres: 42 plates for the caliver (a small arquebuses), 43 for the musket, and last 33 plates for yhe use of pike in infantry tactics.
This work of Jacob De Gheyn result of great importance also for the future great Rembrandt for his master art : The night watch.
A priceless resource for the organization and training of troops, de Gheyn's book created an overnight sensation throughout Europe and was quickly translated into several languages.
An incredible number of imitations editions have since appeared, but *The Exercise of Armes* remains the classic. Above and beyond its intrinsic historic interest, the volume presents a meticulously accurate portrait of uniforms and weapons of the era of Netherlands and Europe, in addition to the aesthetic appeal of its remarkable engravings of this great artist!

WWW.SOLDIERSHOP.COM   SOLDIERS, WEAPONS & UNIFORMS 600- 001

ISBN: 978-88-93271240-2

SWU-600-006

9 788893 271240

SOLDIERSHOP PUBLISHING

THE EXERCISE OF ARMES
JACOB DE GHEYN II - LUCA S. CRISTINI

SOLDIERSHOP PUBLISHING

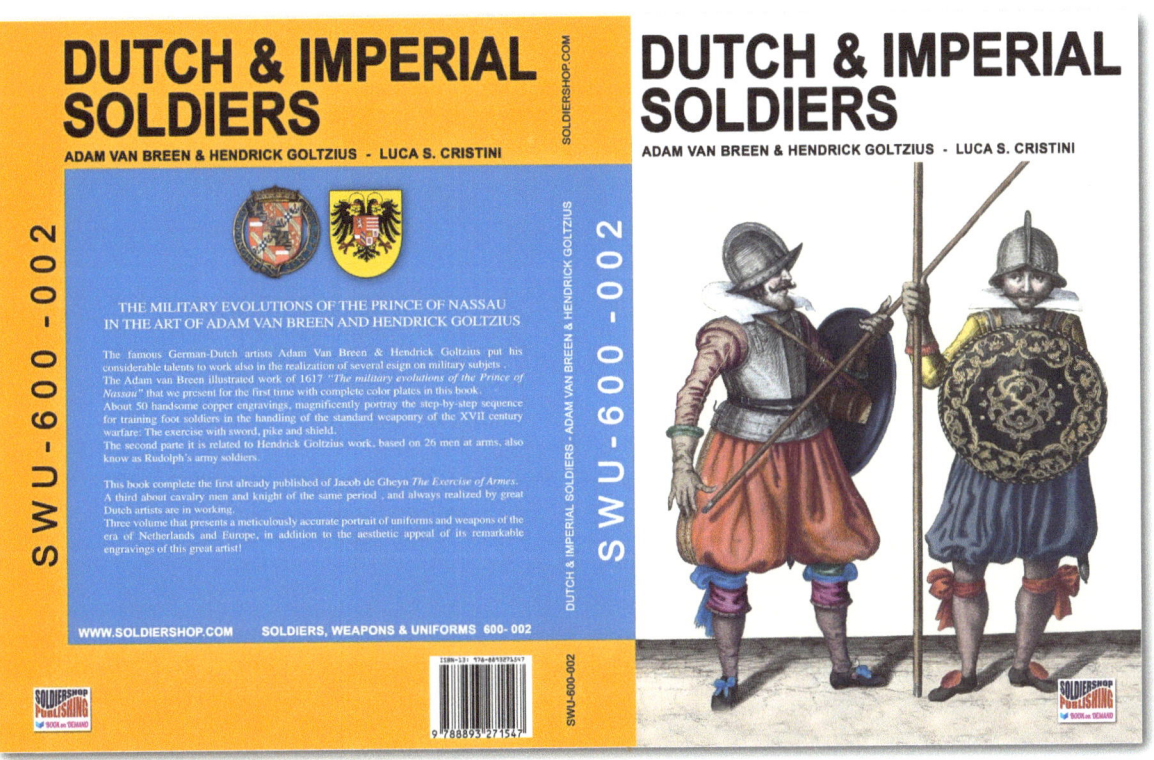

DUTCH & IMPERIAL SOLDIERS
ADAM VAN BREEN & HENDRICK GOLTZIUS - LUCA S. CRISTINI

SWU-600-002

SOLDIERSHOP.COM

DUTCH & IMPERIAL SOLDIERS - ADAM VAN BREEN & HENDRICK GOLTZIUS

SWU-600-002

THE MILITARY EVOLUTIONS OF THE PRINCE OF NASSAU IN THE ART OF ADAM VAN BREEN AND HENDRICK GOLTZIUS

The famous German-Dutch artists Adam Van Breen & Hendrick Goltzius put his considerable talents to work also in the realization of several esign on military subjets .
The Adam van Breen illustrated work of 1617 *"The military evolutions of the Prince of Nassau"* that we present for the first time with complete color plates in this book.
About 50 handsome copper engravings, magnificently portray the step-by-step sequence for training foot soldiers in the handling of the standard weaponry of the XVII century warfare: The exercise with sword, pike and shield.
The second parte it is related to Hendrick Goltzius work, based on 26 men at arms, also know as Rudolph's army soldiers.

This book complete the first already published of Jacob de Gheyo *The Exercise of Armes*. A third about cavalry men and knight of the same period , and always realized by great Dutch artists are in working.
Three volume that presents a meticulously accurate portrait of uniforms and weapons of the era of Netherlands and Europe, in addition to the aesthetic appeal of its remarkable engravings of this great artist!

WWW.SOLDIERSHOP.COM   SOLDIERS, WEAPONS & UNIFORMS 600- 002

ISBN-13: 978-8893271547

SWU-600-002

9 788893 271547

SOLDIERSHOP PUBLISHING

DUTCH & IMPERIAL SOLDIERS
ADAM VAN BREEN & HENDRICK GOLTZIUS - LUCA S. CRISTINI

SOLDIERSHOP PUBLISHING